Sensory Seeking SEBASTIAN

By Christia DeShields   Illustrated by Marissa Nelson

Sensory Seeking Sebastian is a book that empowers sensory seekers with strategies that help with self regulation. Author, Christia DeShields, who has been in the field of education for over 10 years, and her husband, Kenneth, have a son that has ADHD and Proprioceptive Sensory Disorder. They learned these strategies through Occupational Therapy with their sensory seeker. Since learning these strategies, their son takes the initiative to regulate himself, and is now helping others. This book is perfect for families who want to equip their sensory seeker in navigating the challenges of ADHD, Autism, and SPD.

Copyright © 2020 Christia DeShields.
All rights reserved. This book or any portion thereof may not be reproduced or used in any manner whatsoever without the express written permission of the publisher except for the use of brief quotations in a book review.
Printed by Foresight Publishing Co., in the United States of America.

You are fearfully and wonderfully made. You are a masterpiece.

LOVE,
MOM + DAD

Hello!
My name is Sebastian.
It's nice to meet you!

I need to fill my sensory tank, and I heard you do too.

I have lots of wiggles and I need to get them out... so, I stretch and do bear crawls in my body sock.

When I'm in a new place and I'm as nervous as can be, I take a few deep breaths and it really helps calm me.

I have a lot of energy and I like to move, so I ask to be a big helper and my mom says, "I'm so proud of you!"

When I'm sitting in class but I really want to move, I do chair push ups at my table and it feels pretty cool.

I use my hands a lot and I love to feel different textures; but it's important to ask first and make sure I don't touch others.

13

Sometimes I feel ferocious and want to bite like a lion! I ask for a crunchy treat instead—I love carrots! You should try them!
(If there are no carrots around what can you do? I chew my LEGO necklace and that works great too.)

When I need a break from an activity, I jump on the trampoline to calm my mind and my body.

18

I think it's really great that I can be so strong, but when I'm gentle with my friends we get to have more fun.

There are some times when I just need a tight squeeze, so I put my weighted vest on and now I feel real safe and cozy.

22

When it's time to get ready for bed at night, I do yoga and say my prayers so I can sleep tight.

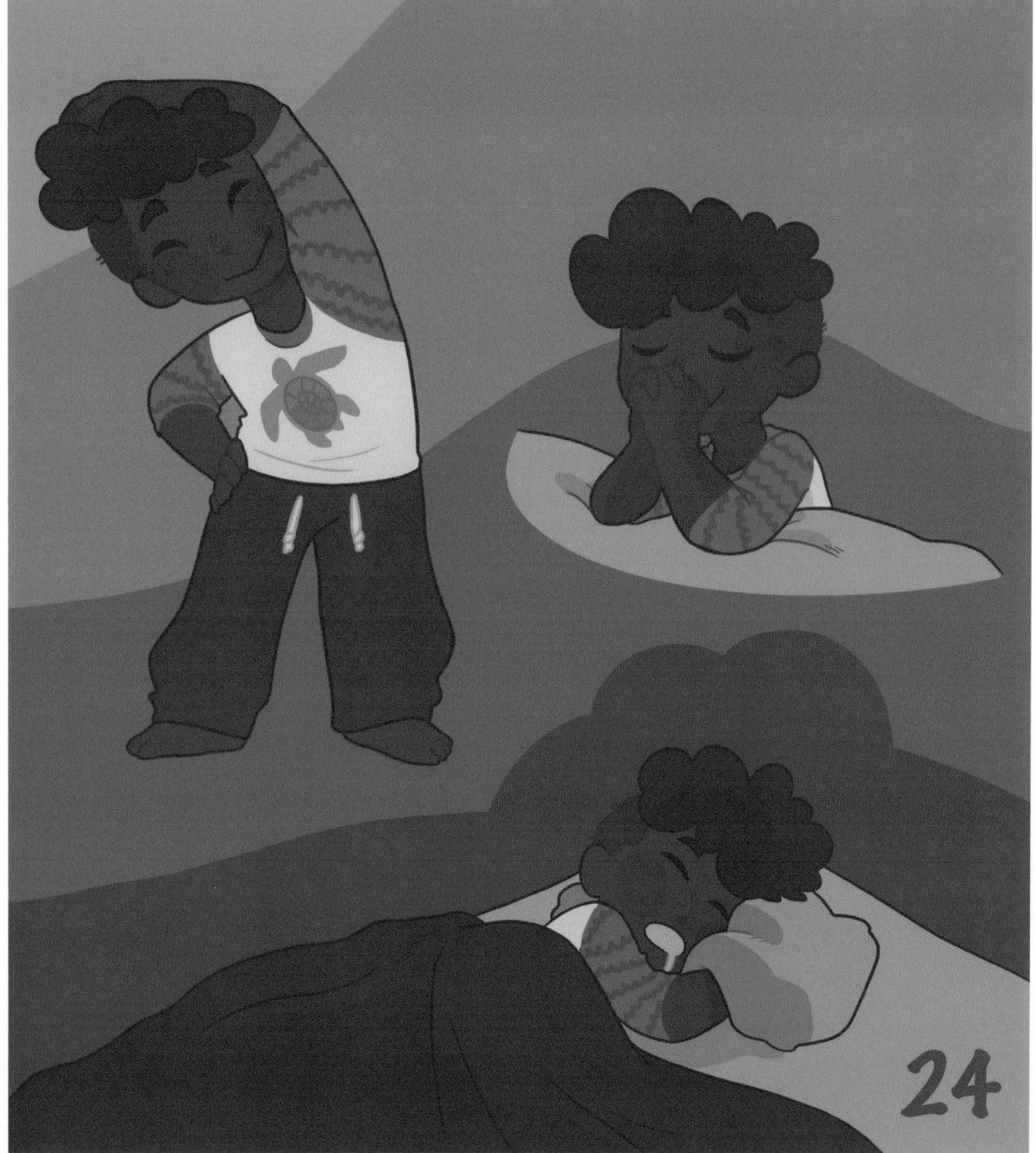

Listening to my body and using my words is the most important thing. If I need to fill my sensory tank, I have to say something.

Here are 20 more ideas to fill your sensory tank:

Swimming
Dancing
Cartwheels
Going down a slide
Squeezing a stress ball
Jumping or crashing into a pillow
Taking a bubble bath
Building blocks
Playing with sand, playdoh, or putty
Chewing gum
Martial Arts
Exercise
Bear crawls
Carrying a heavy backpack or stack of books
Wall push ups
Bear hugs
Pulling resistance bands
Jump in place
Desk stretches
Joint compression

Can you think of a place that makes you feel calm?

How can you get comfortable in a new place?

30

How can you use your words when you need to fill your sensory tank?

Printed in Great Britain
by Amazon